My Big Prayers
The Psalms, Volume 1

A Devotional Prayer Journal
To Help Your Child Develop A Heart For God

Floyd Gary Pierce

For Lily & Ruby

My Big Prayers
Psalms Volume 1

This Devotional Prayer Journal Belongs To

____

I Started This Journal On

____

With

____

Introduction

"Go therefore and make disciples of all nations, baptizing them in the name of the Father and of the Son and of the Holy Spirit, teaching them to observe all that I have commanded you. And behold, I am with you always, to the end of the age."
- Matthew 28:19-20, ESV

DISCIPLESHIP STARTS AT HOME.

Jesus' last words to His followers were to make disciples. The command is as relevant today as it was when He spoke these words. Disciples are followers of Jesus. As a Christian, you are a disciple because you are a follower of Christ. As a follower of Christ, it is up to you to disciple your children. Discipleship starts at home. Parents and grandparents have the primary roles of making disciples. We call this family discipleship.

In his book, "Family Discipleship" (Crossway, p. 24), Matt Chandler writes, "Family discipleship is the important and mostly ordinary spiritual leadership of your home." When you disciple your children, you are doing important work. You may regularly feel you are not making any progress, and you will be tempted to give up. Family discipleship will feel ordinary. You are not attempting to create powerful worship services in your home or develop a thirty-minute sermon each week for your kids. You will intentionally show them what it looks like to follow Jesus. As you show them, you will also need to teach them. Teach them what you were taught. Teach them what you know. Teach them the Bible.

It may feel overwhelming, but you can absolutely do this important and ordinary work. God has equipped you, and you have the promise that Jesus is with you as you do the important ordinary work of making disciples of your children.

In this series of devotional prayer journals, you and your child will work together, learning about who God is from the Bible. You will engage in meaningful conversations about who God is and how your child can follow Him. These journals give you and your child a framework to learn how to pray from the Bible. In the journal, there is an area for your child to express what they understand through a creative activity, along with a place to record answered prayers. You and your child will create a keepsake that you both will treasure for years to come.

How To Use This Book

This devotional prayer journal is for an adult and a preschool to an early elementary-aged child to work through together. There is no right or wrong time of the day to work through this book. Do whatever works best for you and your child. This devotional prayer journal has six sections for each day.

The Bible

Each day starts with a brief psalm from the Bible that focuses on a characteristic of God and will be the foundation of the rest of the journal day. Read the Bible passage to your child. All Bible passages are from the International Children's Bible.

Heart to Heart Devotion

In this section, there is an idea from the Bible explained so that a young child can understand and begin to wonder about God. Read these devotions to your child. Depending on your comfort level with the Bible, you may want to add to these brief devotions.

Questions and Conversations

In this section, the fun begins. These questions will start a conversation between you and your child. Ask your child the questions and let them answer. The hope is that your child begins to wonder about the majesty of our God in this section. Some of their answers may be outlandish or incorrect - that's okay. The goal here is to start the conversation and allow your child to begin to wonder about God.

Prayer Starters

In this section, there are three simple prayer starters for you to show your child how to pray. Talk with them about what prayer is as you start this section. They will soon understand the concept of prayer, but will need help to shape their prayers. That is where these starters come in handy. There is plenty of room for your child to write some of their prayers here. Give your child the pencil, pen, or crayon and let them write in these boxes. Not only will they be able to record their prayers, but you will create a keepsake that you will cherish.

Creative Activity

In this section, there is space for your child to express what you have discussed. For some children, this might be the most enjoyable part of the journal. It will certainly increase the value of the keepsake. These guided creative activities point back to the main idea of the day. Crayons and pencils are best for this section.

Prayers Answered

In this last section, you and your child will record how God has answered your prayers. This will be a visual reminder to you both of how God has been faithful to you. Your first few days may not have much to record, but don't skip it. Use this time to express what faith is and how you trust God, even when you don't see Him working.

Today's Date: __________

God Protects Me

But, Lord, you are my shield.
You are my wonderful God who gives me courage.
I will pray to the Lord.
And he will answer me from his holy mountain.
I can lie down and go to sleep.
And I will wake up again
because the Lord protects me.
    -Psalm 3:3-5

Heart to Heart Devotion

Superheroes have super abilities, like super strength and super speed. They are famous for saving the day and beating the bad guy. Superheroes rescue people from really scary situations. Some superheroes have special tools to help them save the day; tools like a shield.

God is so much better than superheroes. God doesn't need special tools. God protects you with Himself.

This psalm tells us that God is our shield. Shields protect us from things hurting us. Shields can save people from scary situations. God protects us from things that can hurt us. God can save us from scary situations. God loves you more than any superhero could and He can protect you better, too.

Questions and Conversations

Do you know of any superheroes who use a shield?

What do you think a shield does for people who have them?

How can God be our shield?

Prayer Starters

God, You are ...

God, thank You ...

God, I pray ...

Creative Activity

Draw a picture of a shield protecting our family or your friends.

Prayers Answered

My Big Prayers

Today's Date: ___________

God is Strong

Answer me when I pray to you,
my God who does what is right.
Lift the load that I carry.
Be kind to me and hear my prayer.
    - Psalm 4:1

Heart to Heart Devotion

God is strong. God is stronger than the strongest person you know. He can carry the heaviest thing you can think of. In fact, he can carry more than all the heaviest things you can think of all at the same time. God is strong. Have you ever tried to carry something heavy? It's not a problem with God. God can carry it.

Because God is strong, God can help us be strong. When we don't feel strong, we can pray to God. God's strength helps us to be strong when we are sad or worried, too. God's strength can help us to be happy when we are sad. God is strong.

     discipleshipstudio.com

Questions and Conversations

What is the heaviest thing you can think of?

What is the heaviest thing you have ever carried or picked up?

Do you think it is easy for God to carry something heavy? Why?

Prayer Starters

God, You are ...

God, thank You ...

God, I pray ...

Creative Activity

Draw someone you know trying to carry something really heavy.

Prayers Answered

My Big Prayers

Today's Date: __________

God Hears Me When I am Sad

Lord, listen to my words.
Understand what I am thinking.
Listen to my cry for help.
My king and my God, I pray to you.
Lord, every morning you hear my voice.
Every morning, I tell you what I need.
And I wait for your answer.
   - Psalm 5:1-3

Heart to Heart Devotion

   There are times when we are sad, and we just have to cry. Maybe you were sad today, and you cried. That's okay. It's part of being a kid. There are other times when we are happy, and we just have to smile or giggle. You probably smiled today. But when we are sad, we want someone to help us make everything better.

   God hears you when you are sad. God is listening to you all the time. He even knows if you are thinking sad thoughts. If you are ever so sad that you just have to cry, remember that God is listening and can hear you cry. Even if no one else knows you are sad, God knows. You can run to God the next time you are sad and cry to him through prayer. God listens and will hear you when you are sad.

Questions and Conversations

When was the last time you cried? Was it a happy cry or a sad cry?

Why would someone cry to God?

Why does God hear us when we cry to Him?

Prayer Starters

God, You are ...

God, thank You ...

God, I pray ...

Creative Activity

Draw a picture of a crying ear.

Prayers Answered

Prayers Answered

Today's Date: ___________

God Loves Me

Because of your great love,
I can come into your Temple.
Because I fear and respect you,
I can worship in your holy Temple.
- Psalm 5:7

Heart to Heart Devotion

God loves you. He loves you very much. In fact, God loves you more than anyone else can ever love you, because He is God. Yes, your family loves you a bunch. They love you more than you can imagine, but God's love for you is even more.

When someone loves you, they want to spend time with you. They want to hear you. They want you to know they care. When someone loves you, they want to give you things. They want to be close to you. You understand that when you see how much your family loves you. You can trust that is true with God, too. God tells us He loves us many times and in many ways in the Bible.

God shows us that He loves us by sending Jesus to rescue us. John 3:16 says, "For God loved the world so much that he gave his only Son. God gave his Son so that whoever believes in him may not be lost, but have eternal life." Now say this verse with your name instead of "the world." That's how much God loves you.

                    discipleshipstudio.com

Questions and Conversations

Who are some people who love you?

How big is God's love for you?

How can we love God?

Prayer Starters

God, You are ...

God, thank You ...

God, I pray ...

My Big Prayers

Creative Activity

Draw a picture of a big heart with you in the middle and write "God loves me" under the heart.

 discipleshipstudio.com

Prayers Answered

My Big Prayers

Today's Date: ____________

God Makes Me Happy

But let everyone who trusts you be happy.
Let them sing glad songs forever.
Protect those who love you.
They are happy because of you.
    - Psalm 5:11

Heart to Heart Devotion

Think of a time that you were so happy that you just had to sing. Maybe it was today. Being happy makes us smile. It can make us sing and maybe even dance. Everything feels great when we are happy. We love being happy. Being happy is so much fun.

God makes us happy. Because of the happiness that comes from loving God and being loved by God, we sing. Sometimes we dance and clap our hands. This happiness will last forever! It will be so much fun singing and dancing forever because of God. God makes us so happy that we will never get tired of singing about His love for us.

     discipleshipstudio.com

Questions and Conversations

What makes you happy? Why?

What is that happiest song you have ever heard?

How does God make you happy?

Prayer Starters

God, You are ...

God, thank You ...

God, I pray ...

Creative Activity

Draw a picture of our family singing a happy song.

Prayers Answered

My Big Prayers

Today's Date: ____________

God Does What is Right

God, you do what is right.
I praise the Lord because he does what is right.
I sing praises to the name of the Lord Most High.
    - Psalm 7:9a, 17

Heart to Heart Devotion

God is busy at work in our family and in our church. God is busy at work in the world, too. He is always doing many things all at once. In all His busyness, He never makes a mistake. Never. God always does the right thing.

It's hard for you and me to always do the right thing. Maybe we do the right thing some of the time or maybe even most of the time. But sometimes, we do the wrong thing. We just do, even when we don't want to. We are not perfect.

God never ever does the wrong thing. He always does what should be done. He always does it the right way. God is perfect.

     discipleshipstudio.com

Questions and Conversations

What do you think it means to be right?

What do you think it means to be wrong?

Why does God always do what is right?

Prayer Starters

God, You are ...

God, thank You ...

God, I pray ...

Creative Activity

Draw a picture of a friend teaching you something right.

Prayers Answered

My Big Prayers

Today's Date: ____________

God's Name is the
Most Wonderful Name

Lord our Master,
your name is the most wonderful name
in all the earth!
It brings you praise in heaven above.
   - Psalm 8:1

Heart to Heart Devotion

   Everyone loves to hear their name spoken by other people. We also love to write our names down. Sometimes grown ups will have their name on their door or on their desk. Our name helps people know who we are. Our name tells people a little bit about us.

   When we hear our name in a crowd, we will turn around to see who said it because they might want to tell us something. Our name is important to us. When someone asks, "Who are you?" We usually say our name. God's name is important, too. God's name says a lot about Him. It says that He made everything and that He is in control of things. It says so much to us. When we hear God's name, we know God loves us and cares for us. We know that He protects us and hears us when we pray. God's name is the best name ever because His name tells us about Him.

   discipleshipstudio.com

Questions and Conversations

What do you like about your name?

If you could change your name, what would it be? Why?

Why do you think God's name is the most wonderful name in all the earth?

Prayer Starters

God, You are ...

God, thank You ...

God, I pray ...

Creative Activity

Draw a picture of a your name and decorate it.

Prayers Answered

Today's Date: ____________

God Thinks I am Important

But why is man important to you?
Why do you take care of human beings?
You made man a little lower than the angels. And
you crowned him with glory and honor.
You put him in charge of everything you made.
You put all things under his control:
all the sheep, the cattle and the wild animals,
the birds in the sky, the fish in the sea, and
everything that lives under water.
   - Psalm 8:4-8

Heart to Heart Devotion

So far in our time together in this book, we have discovered how God protects us, loves us, and makes us happy. God takes care of us, too. He takes care of us like how a mommy bird takes care of her baby birds, or like how a daddy elephant takes care of his baby elephants. God takes care of us like your parents and grandparents take care of you. God takes care of you because you are important to Him.

Remember that God loves you. He sent Jesus to rescue you. He did that because you are important to Him. You matter to God and you always will.

Questions and Conversations

Why do you think God takes care of us?

Why are we so important to God?

How does this make God so wonderful?

Prayer Starters

God, You are ...

God, thank You ...

God, I pray ...

Creative Activity

Draw a picture of you playing with your favorite animals.

Prayers Answered

My Big Prayers

Today's Date: __________

God is a Helpful King

But the Lord rules forever.
He sits on his throne to judge.
The Lord will judge the world by what is right.
He will decide what is fair for the nations.
The Lord defends those who suffer.
He protects them in times of trouble.
Those who know the Lord trust him.
He will not leave those who come to him.
    - Psalm 9:7-10

Heart to Heart Devotion

A king is the boss or leader of a group of people. A king gets to make the rules and make sure that everyone follows the rules. Kings are in charge.

God is a king. God is the leader of everyone but especially those who follow after Him. God gets to make the rules. We can find His rules in the Bible. God gets to make sure everyone follows the rules. God is in charge. God makes sure we are safe. God is different than other kings because God is a helpful king.

God loves His people more than any king could love his people. God is more powerful than any other king. God helps those who follow Him. God is a helpful king.

     discipleshipstudio.com

Questions and Conversations

How do you help around the house?

What does a king do? Haw can a king be helpful?

How do you think God can help you?

Prayer Starters

God, You are ...

God, thank You ...

God, I pray ...

Creative Activity

Draw a picture of a king sitting on a throne.

Prayers Answered

Today's Date: ___________

God is Kind

Lord, be kind to me.
  - Psalm 9:13a

Heart to Heart Devotion

Kindness is the happy way to live with friends, family, and others. Sharing what you have, saying nice things to each other, and offering to help someone who needs help are all kind ways to live. We love when people are kind to us.

God is kind. God is the best at being kind, because no one can be as kind as God. God is super kind. He doesn't just share with you, He gives you everything. He doesn't just say nice things to you, He knows you and loves you. He doesn't help you when you need help, He sent Jesus to rescue you. God is the kindest kind of kind.

You have friends who are kind to you, but then at times, they can also be mean to you. You have probably tried to be kind at times, but you know that sometimes you are not feeling kind and you are selfish or unkind. God is always kind. He never feels selfish or unkind. God is kind.

    discipleshipstudio.com

Questions and Conversations

How has a friend shown kindness to you?

What are some ways God show kindness to our family?

How can you show kindness to others?

Prayer Starters

God, You are ...

God, thank You ...

God, I pray ...

Creative Activity

Draw a picture of you being kind to a friend.

Prayers Answered

My Big Prayers

God Hears Me When I am Hurting

The Lord is King forever and ever.
Remove from your land those nations that do not
worship you.
Lord, you have heard what the poor people want.
Do what they ask. Listen to them.
Protect the orphans. Put an end to suffering.
Then they will no longer be afraid of evil people.
    - Psalm 10:16-18

Heart to Heart Devotion

   God is King forever. He will never not be King. God is a good King who hears you when you pray to Him. God listens to you and to others when we pray to Him. You can pray to Him when you are happy or when you are sad. It is good to pray to God no matter how you are feeling.

   God wants to hear from you when you are happy. God wants to hear from you when you are sad or hurting, too. Not only does God hear you, but He also helps you when you pray to Him. You can pray to God when others are hurting or sad. It is good to pray for your friends or family members. God wants to hear those prayers. God is a good King who hears you when you pray.

Questions and Conversations

How can God help us when we are hurting?

How do you think God can make things better when we are sad?

Prayer Starters

God, You are ...

God, thank You ...

God, I pray ...

Creative Activity

Draw a picture of a hurting ear.

Prayers Answered

Today's Date: ___________

God Sees Me

The Lord is in his holy temple.
The Lord sits on his throne in heaven.
And he sees what people do.
He keeps his eye on them.
    - Psalm 11:4

Heart to Heart Devotion

God is a good King. He is a powerful King. He is a King who can see you from His throne. If you were to look out of your window in the middle of the day, how far could you see? If you were to look out your window in the middle of the night, how far could you see? God sees you and it doesn't matter if it is night or day.

When you love someone, you want to see them. God loves you and wants to see you. He thinks you are very special and loves to watch over you just to see you and it doesn't matter if it is day or night, clear or cloudy. God sees you because He loves you.

Questions and Conversations

When you look out your window, how far can you see?

How do you think God can see what we do?

Can God see us all the time?

Prayer Starters

God, You are ...

God, thank You ...

God, I pray ...

Creative Activity

Draw a picture of a really big eye.

Prayers Answered

My Big Prayers

Today's Date: ____________

God Helps Me

But the Lord says,
"I will now rise up
because the poor are being hurt.
Because of the moans of the helpless,
I will give them the help they want."
- Psalm 12:5

Heart to Heart Devotion

God helps you when you need help. He is such a helpful God. There really is no one like our God, because He is all-powerful and He loves you. God has the power to help you when you pray to Him. When you need help, you can pray to God and ask Him to help you. He loves you and loves to help you.

God loves to help your friends and family, too. If you know that one of your friends or family members needs some help, you can ask God to help them. God says that He will help people who are being hurt. He will help those who can't help themselves. God is such a good God.

     discipleshipstudio.com

Questions and Conversations

How can God help you?

How can God help your friends?

How can God help our family?

Prayer Starters

God, You are ...

God, thank You ...

God, I pray ...

Creative Activity

Draw a picture of you helping a friend.

Prayers Answered

Today's Date: ___________

God Saves Me

I trust in your love.
My heart is happy because you saved me.
I sing to the Lord
because he has taken care of me.
    - Psalm 13:5-6

Heart to Heart Devotion

   God loves you! When your family tells you they love you, do you believe them? Sure, you do, because you can trust them. They show you they love you by spending time with you and helping you. When you see your family after they come home from school or work, you are happy because you love them too.

   God loves you and He saves you. God shows you that He loves you so much that He sent His Son, Jesus. Jesus rescues you when you needed the most help. God really does save you and takes care of you. As you get older and understand how much God has saved you, your love for God will grow bigger and bigger. God loves you and saves you.

Questions and Conversations

How does God take care of you?

How has God saved you?

What does a happy heart feel like? Why do you think happy hearts sing?

Prayer Starters

God, You are ...

God, thank You ...

God, I pray ...

Creative Activity

Draw a picture of a happy heart singing to God.

Prayers Answered

My Big Prayers

Today's Date: __________

God is Special

Lord, who may enter your Holy Tent?
Who may live on your holy mountain?
Only a person who is innocent
and who does what is right.
He must speak the truth from his heart.
   - Psalm 15:1-2

Heart to Heart Devotion

   God is special because He is different than us. He is God. God created everything. Since God is our creator, He gets to make the rules. His rules say that only a perfect person can approach Him.

   Jesus is special because He is the only perfect person. Sometimes we aren't perfect. We might lie, even just a little bit. We might try to hurt someone, even our friends. We might break a promise, even if we just forgot. But not Jesus. He always tells the truth. He never hurts his friends and He keeps every promise.

   We need Jesus everyday. Jesus is God's Son. Jesus is special and helps us love God. Jesus is a gift from God. The Bible says, *"For God loved the world so much that he gave his only Son. God gave his Son so that whoever believes in him may not be lost, but have eternal life."* (John 3:16)

     discipleshipstudio.com

Questions and Conversations

Is there anyone who always tells the truth, never hurts his friends, and keeps every promise?

Jesus is the only one who can do all of this. What do you know about Jesus?

Prayer Starters

God, You are ...

God, thank You ...

God, I pray ...

Creative Activity

Draw a picture of a cross.

Prayers Answered

Today's Date: ___________

Good Things Come From God

Protect me, God,
because I trust in you.
I said to the Lord, "You are my Lord.
Every good thing I have comes from you."
There are godly people in the world.
I enjoy them.
    - Psalm 16:1-3

Heart to Heart Devotion

   Did you know that you are trusting something every time you sit down? When you sit down in a chair, you are trusting that the chair will hold you up. When you trust something or someone, it is more than just believing something about them. You are doing something because you believe something. You sit in the chair because you believe it will hold you up.

   Trusting God is kind of like that. When you trust God, you are doing something because you believe He won't let you down. We can trust God because He is so good to us. He gives us good things. The Bible says that every good thing comes from God.

   Some of those good gifts that God gives us are other people in our lives. God loves you so much, that He has placed some really great people in your life to love you and help you love God.

          discipleshipstudio.com

Questions and Conversations

What does it mean to trust in God?

What are some good things you have? Those things came from God.

Who are some people you love?

Prayer Starters

God, You are ...

God, thank You ...

God, I pray ...

Creative Activity

Draw a picture of some of your favorite things or people.

Prayers Answered

My Big Prayers

Today's Date: ____________

God is All I Need

No, the Lord is all I need.
He takes care of me.
My share in life has been pleasant.
My part has been beautiful.
I praise the Lord because he guides me.
Even at night, I feel his leading.
So I rejoice, and I am glad. Even my body has hope.
   - Psalm 16:5-7, 9

Heart to Heart Devotion

Hope is when we expect something good to happen. We can hope for pancakes for breakfast or a new toy for our birthday. Those would be good, wouldn't they? We can also hope in God when we love and trust Him. God is always with you, He will never leave you. You can always pray to Him and trust Him.

The Bible says that God is all we need. God is so good to us. When we love and follow after God, we have everything we need. He gives us all the good things we need. God gives us our home. God gives us our food. God gives us our friends. God is really good to us, isn't He?

When we love and follow after God, we have all that we need, because we have God and we can trust God.

     discipleshipstudio.com

Questions and Conversations

How would you describe hope?

How is God always with you?

Why do you think God is all you need?

Prayer Starters

God, You are ...

God, thank You ...

God, I pray ...

Creative Activity

Draw a picture of a time when you were happy.

Prayers Answered

Today's Date: ___________

God is My Rock

I love you, Lord. You are my strength.
The Lord is my rock, my protection, my Savior.
My God is my rock.
I can run to him for safety.
He is my shield and my saving strength, my high tower.
I will call to the Lord.
He is worthy of praise.
And I will be saved from my enemies.
    - Psalm 18:1-3

Heart to Heart Devotion

God is strong. Because He is strong, He makes us stronger when we need help. We are strong because God is strong. He gives us strength. Because He is strong, God is like a really big rock that protects us.

Have you ever tried to protect a toy or a pet? It's hard to protect something we love sometimes. It is no problem for God. He can protect you, our family, and your friends. God is like a really big rock out in the ocean. Even though waves crash up against it, the rock is not moved. God is a rock that cannot be moved, especially when He is protecting you.

Questions and Conversations

Have you ever seen a really big rock? What was it like?

What do you think it means that God is your rock?

What does God save us from?

Prayer Starters

God, You are ...

God, thank You ...

God, I pray ...

Creative Activity

Draw a picture of a small rock being protected by a really big rock.

Prayers Answered

My Big Prayers

God Hears My Prayers

Lord, hear me begging for fairness.
Listen to my cry for help.
Pay attention to my prayer.
I speak the truth.
I call to you, God,
and you answer me.
Listen to me now.
Hear what I say.
   - Psalm 17:1,6

Heart to Heart Devotion

   "That's not fair!" Have you ever said that? Probably. We all have said it at some point in our life. We want the right things to be done and the wrong things to be undone. That's fair. We can ask God to make the right things done and the wrong things undone. When we talk to God, we are praying to Him.

   When we pray to God, we can do it out loud like He is in the room with us. We can also pray to God in our minds. We can think our prayers to God. Sometimes we may not know what to say or how to say it. God knows what we need or want anyway. He is God.

   No matter how we pray, we can know that God hears our prayers. If our prayers are happy prayers or sad prayers, God hears them. God hears you when you pray.

 discipleshipstudio.com

Questions and Conversations

What do you think it means to be fair?

How do you call out to God?

Why do you think God hears our prayers?

Prayer Starters

God, You are ...

God, thank You ...

God, I pray ...

My Big Prayers

Creative Activity

Draw a picture of super silly picture of someone trying to call God on a phone.

 discipleshipstudio.com

Prayers Answered

Today's Date: ___________

God is Good

Lord, you are loyal to those who are loyal.
You are good to those who are good.
You are pure to those who are pure.
But you are against those who are bad.
You save those who are not proud.
But you make humble those who are proud.
Lord, you give light to my lamp.
My God brightens the darkness around me.
    - Psalm 18:25-28

Heart to Heart Devotion

    God is a really good friend, especially when we are a good friend to God. God is the best friend we can have. He keeps His promises to us. He is good to us. He never lies to us. God is good. God is the best kind of good.

    God saves us from trouble. He gives us light in the darkness. In fact, the Bible describes God as being light. God is so good He brings light into the darkness. We have a really good God, don't we?

Questions and Conversations

What are some good think you have done for a friend or your family?

What are some things that make God good?

Prayer Starters

God, You are ...

God, thank You ...

God, I pray ...

My Big Prayers

Creative Activity

Draw a picture of you doing something good for a friend.

 discipleshipstudio.com

Prayers Answered

Today's Date: __________

God Doesn't Make Mistakes

The ways of God are without fault.
The Lord's words are pure.
He is a shield to those who trust him.
Who is God? Only the Lord.
Who is the Rock? Only our God.
God is my protection.
He makes my way free from fault.
He makes me like a deer, which does not stumble.
He helps me stand on the steep mountains.
    - Psalms 18:30-33

Heart to Heart Devotion

God doesn't need an eraser. He never makes mistakes. God didn't make a mistake when He made you. He didn't make a mistake when He put our family together. God doesn't make mistakes.

Have you ever had to scribble out something on a drawing you were making? Everyone has. But God never needs to scribble or start over.

This is really true when it comes to what God tells us in the Bible. God's words in the Bible are pure. That means there is no mistake in them. When God says He loves you in the Bible, He means it. When God says He will protect His people, He will. God can be trusted, because God doesn't make mistakes.

     discipleshipstudio.com

Questions and Conversations

What are God's words?

Why do you think the Bible is pure?

Prayer Starters

God, You are ...

God, thank You ...

God, I pray ...

Creative Activity

Draw a picture of a Bible.

Prayers Answered

Prayers Answered

Today's Date: ___________

God Should Be Worshipped

So I will praise you, Lord, among the nations.
I will sing praises to your name.
The Lord gives great victories to his king.
He is loyal to his appointed king,
to David and his descendants forever.
    - Psalms 18:49-50

Heart to Heart Devotion

   What do you get most excited about? How do you feel when you think about it? Those feelings are what people feel when they think about God. People who know God, love God. Their love for God makes them want to sing about Him.

   This is called praising God. When we praise God, we sing about Him, talk about Him, pray to Him, and even dance because of Him. We do it because it is a way to show God we love Him. He loves us so much, we want to do something to show Him we love Him, so we praise God.

   God is so good, He deserves our praise. God has done and continues to do so many great things, that it is good to praise Him.

Questions and Conversations

Do you have a favorite praise song? If so, what is it?

Why do you think we sing songs to God?

What is something about God you could praise God for?

Prayer Starters

God, You are ...

God, thank You ...

God, I pray ...

Creative Activity

Sing your favorite praise song to God. Write some of the lyrics to the song.

Prayers Answered

Today's Date: __________

God Created the Sky

The heavens tell the glory of God.
And the skies announce what his hands have made.
Day after day they tell the story.
Night after night they tell it again.
They have no speech or words.
They don't make any sound to be heard.
But their message goes out through all the world.
It goes everywhere on earth.
The sky is like a home for the sun.
    - Psalm 19:1-4

Heart to Heart Devotion

    When you look up at the night sky, what do you see? There are stars, planets, moons, and galaxies. God created all those things.

    Galaxies are huge groups of stars. God created each of the stars and each of the galaxies. Some of those stars have planets around them. Some of those planets have moons. Each of them tell us that God deserves our praise.

    Everything we can see in the night sky tells a story about how God is a good creator. They don't say a word. They don't have to, they are there because God created them. If they could speak, they would join us in praising God. God is a good creator.

         discipleshipstudio.com

Questions and Conversations

What does the sky tells us about God?

How can you tell a story about God without using words?

Prayer Starters

God, You are ...

God, thank You ...

God, I pray ...

Creative Activity

Draw a picture of the sky telling a story about God.

Prayers Answered

My Big Prayers

God's Words are True

The Lord's teachings are perfect.
They give new strength.
The Lord's rules can be trusted.
They make plain people wise.
They are worth more than gold,
even the purest gold.
They are sweeter than honey,
even the finest honey.
    - Psalm 19:7, 10

Heart to Heart Devotion

   The Bible is perfect and can make you stronger in your love for God. You can always trust God and the Bible. He will never lie to you. When you are able to read on your own, you should read the Bible everyday because you will know more about God.

   God's Words are true and pure. When you read them they will make you happy because they tell you about the God who loves you and created you. God's Words are so good, they are better than candy. Can you believe that? God's Words are sweeter than candy and worth more than all the money in the world.

Questions and Conversations

How can the Bible make us stronger?

What is your favorite candy? Why do you love it?

Prayer Starters

God, You are ...

God, thank You ...

God, I pray ...

Creative Activity

Draw a picture of your favorite candy and remember the Bible is better than candy.

Prayers Answered

Today's Date: ____________

God is a Friendly King

Poor people will eat until they are full.
Those who look to the Lord will praise him.
May your hearts live forever!
People everywhere will remember
and will turn to the Lord.
All the families of the nations will worship him.
This is because the Lord is King.
He rules the nations.
All the powerful people on earth will eat and
worship.
Everyone will bow down to him.
   - Psalm 22:26-29

Heart to Heart Devotion

   Who are some of your best friends? What makes them best friends? It is good to have so many people you can count on. It is good to be there for them when they need you. God is a great best friend. He is the best best friend.

   God hears you when you need Him. God listens to you. God helps those who are his friends. God is such a good friend because He loves you. God is a good friend to have because He is able to do things that your other friends are not be able to do. Are any of your other friends kings or queens? God is King. God is so good. He deserves to be praised because He is the friendly king.

     discipleshipstudio.com

Questions and Conversations

What does it mean to worship God?

Why is it so important for us to worship God?

How is God the best best friend?

Prayer Starters

God, You are ...

God, thank You ...

God, I pray ...

Creative Activity

Draw a picture of a friendly king.

Prayers Answered

Today's Date: __________

God Takes Care of Me

The Lord is my shepherd.
I have everything I need.
He gives me rest in green pastures.
He leads me to calm water.
He gives me new strength.
For the good of his name,
he leads me on paths that are right.
Even if I walk through a very dark valley,
I will not be afraid because you are with me.
Your rod and your walking stick comfort me.
   - Psalm 23:1-4

Heart to Heart Devotion

When you need help putting your shoes on, you know your family will help you. When you need help cleaning up your room, you know your family is there for you. As you grow and get older, you will be able to do more stuff without your family's help. But you will never outgrow your need for God's help.

God is always there to help you. God takes care of you like many families care for a pet. God really helps you when you are afraid. The next time you are afraid, remember that God is with you and He takes care of you. Since God is strong and powerful, we can trust that God can take care of us when we are afraid.

Questions and Conversations

How does God take care of our family?

Why do we not need to be afraid if God is with us?

Prayer Starters

God, You are ...

God, thank You ...

God, I pray ...

Creative Activity

Draw a picture of someone who is not afraid.

 discipleshipstudio.com

Prayers Answered

Today's Date: ___________

God is a Warrior

The earth and everything in it belong to the Lord.
The world and all its people belong to him.
Who is this glorious king?
The Lord, strong and mighty.
The Lord, the powerful warrior.
Open up, you gates.
Open wide, you aged doors.
Then the glorious king will come in.
Who is this glorious king?
The Lord of heaven's armies—
he is the glorious king.
  - Psalm 24:1, 8-10

Heart to Heart Devotion

You belong to God because He created you. God is a good creator. He loves what He made. God loves you. God knows that sometimes we don't love Him. This happens when we do things that God doesn't like. It's called sin and it makes God sad. God doesn't stay sad with us. Because He loves us so much, He comes after us to bring us back to Him.

God fights for those He loves. He fights for you. He is strong and mighty. He is a powerful warrior. When He fights, He wins. God always wins.

     discipleshipstudio.com

Questions and Conversations

Why does everything belong to God?

If God is a strong, mighty, and powerful warrior, who does God fight for?

Prayer Starters

God, You are ...

God, thank You ...

God, I pray ...

Questions and Conversations

What does God use to tell us how to live?

How can we use the Bible to live the way God wants us to live?

Prayer Starters

God, You are …

God, thank You …

God, I pray …

My Big Prayers

Creative Activity

Draw a picture of an army protecting the world.

My Big Prayers

Today's Date: ___________

God Shows Me the Way

Lord, tell me your ways.
Show me how to live.
Guide me in your truth.
Teach me, my God, my Savior.
I trust you all day long.
Lord, remember your mercy and love.
You have shown them since long ago.
Do not remember the sins
and wrong things I did when I was young.
But remember to love me always
because you are good, Lord.
  - Psalm 25:4-7

Heart to Heart Devotion

As you get older, you will do lots of things that you can't do now. Some of those things will be hard, some will be easy. You will be able to do things you have seen your family do. God will be with you through it.

God shows you the way, especially when you don't know which way to go. You can trust God's leading. You can find the way God leads in the Bible. Read the Bible to know how God wants you to go. God teaches you in the Bible. When you know God through the Bible, you will be able to do things that please God.

Creative Activity

Draw a picture of someone reading the Bible.

Prayers Answered

Today's Date: ___________

God is Always Good and Right

The Lord is good and right.
He points sinners to the right way.
He shows those who are not proud how to do right.
He teaches them his ways.
All the Lord's ways are loving and true
for those who follow
the demands of his agreement.
For the sake of your name, Lord,
forgive my many sins.
    - Psalm 25:8-11

Heart to Heart Devotion

    God is always good. That's good to know. We have a good God. We have a God who is never wrong. He is always right.

    When we read the Bible, we have an always good and always right God speaking. When we follow God from the Bible, we know that we have a loving God who is true to us. He will always lead us in the right way. He would never lead us in the wrong direction.

    Always look to God and the Bible and you will see our good and right God.

Questions and Conversations

What are some ways that we know God is good?

How does God love us?

Prayer Starters

God, You are ...

God, thank You ...

God, I pray ...

Creative Activity

Draw a picture of someone looking for help.

Prayers Answered

My Big Prayers

Today's Date: ___________

God Keeps Me Safe

The Lord is my light and the one who saves me.
So why should I fear anyone?
The Lord protects my life.
So why should I be afraid?
Evil people may try to destroy my body.
My enemies and those who hate me attack me.
But they are overwhelmed and defeated.
If an army surrounds me,
I will not be afraid.
If war breaks out,
I will trust the Lord.
   - Psalm 27:1-3

Heart to Heart Devotion

   You will never be in a place where God can't save you. He is always with you. He is powerful and mighty. Even if you are in a scary place, God is there with you. When you know that God is with you, you don't have to be afraid.

   God is kind of like a big strong fort. When you are inside that fort, you are protected and safe. The Bible helps you remember this, it helps you stay in the fort. When you are scared, you can hide in the powerful strong fort of God and not worry or be afraid.

     discipleshipstudio.com

Questions and Conversations

What does God save us from?

How can we trust God when we are afraid?

Prayer Starters

God, You are ...

God, thank You ...

God, I pray ...

My Big Prayers

Creative Activity

Draw a picture of a fort with big walls protecting our family.

Prayers Answered

My Big Prayers

Today's Date: ____________

God Makes Me Very Happy

Praise the Lord. He heard my prayer for help.
The Lord is my strength and shield.
I trust him, and he helps me. I am very happy.
And I praise him with my song.
The Lord is powerful.
He gives power and victory to his chosen one.
Save your people. Bless those who are your own.
Be their shepherd and carry them forever.
    - Psalm 28:6-9

Heart to Heart Devotion

    A blessing is a good gift from God. You don't do anything to deserve the blessing. You might even be surprised by the blessing. A blessing, even when it is unexpected will make you happy. It is a good gift from God.

    People who love and follow God will receive many types of good gifts from God. God gives blessings to His people because He cares for them, kind of like how a shepherd takes care of sheep. The shepherds only job is to care for sheep. The shepherd will make sure there is food for the sheep. He will protect the sheep at night. The shepherd cares very much for his sheep.

    God is always caring for His people and His care for you will make you very happy.

 discipleshipstudio.com

Questions and Conversations

What are some blessings in your life?

How does a shepherd care for sheep?

Prayer Starters

God, You are ...

God, thank You ...

God, I pray ...

My Big Prayers

Creative Activity

Draw a picture of a shepherd caring for a sheep.

Prayers Answered

Today's Date: ____________

God is Wonderful

Praise the Lord, you angels.
Praise the Lord's glory and power.
Praise the Lord for the glory of his name.
Worship the Lord because he is holy.
In his Temple everyone says, "Glory to God!"
    - Psalm 29:1-2, 9b

Heart to Heart Devotion

Angels are real and they praise God, just like you and me. God created the angels, just like He created everything else. Angels get to be around God all the time. How much fun is that? The angels are around God so much, they can't help but to praise Him.

Angels get to see what God is doing in ways we are not able to see yet. They are God's messengers. In the Bible, there are many stories of angels coming to earth with a message from God for someone. These messages can be hard to believe, but since they come from God, they can be believed. God can be trusted.

God gets praise from the angels and humans who follow Him. One way humans praise God is by saying, "Glory to God!" Let's say it together, "Glory to God!"

   discipleshipstudio.com

Questions and Conversations

How do you think angels praise God?

What do you think "Glory to God" means?

Prayer Starters

God, You are ...

God, thank You ...

God, I pray ...

My Big Prayers

Creative Activity

Draw a picture of an angel praising God.

Prayers Answered

My Big Prayers

God Rescues Me

I will praise you, Lord,
because you rescued me.
You did not let my enemies laugh at me.
Lord, my God, I prayed to you.
And you healed me.
You lifted me out of the grave.
You spared me from going down where the dead are.
Sing praises to the Lord, you who belong to him.
Praise his holy name.
   - Psalm 30:1-4

Heart to Heart Devotion

   God is holy because He does work that only He can do. God created us to do holy work with Him, but our sin keeps us from doing what God wants us to do. Sin is when we think or do things that God doesn't want us to think or do. God doesn't like sin. He knows that everybody sins. He still wants us to do holy work, so he rescues and heals us from our sin.

   As God rescues us, He keeps us from getting the punishment our sin deserves. This is great news. We sing songs about how good God is to rescue us from our sin. When we follow Jesus, we are able to do holy work again with God. We can praise God with song and dance.

Questions and Conversations

What do you think holy means?

How can God take someone who is sad and make them happy?

Prayer Starters

God, You are ...

God, thank You ...

God, I pray ...

Creative Activity

Draw a picture of sad person getting happy and dancing.

Prayers Answered

My Big Prayers

God Leads Me

Lord, I trust in you.
Let me never be disgraced.
Save me because you do what is right.
Listen to me.
Save me quickly.
Be my rock of protection,
a strong city to save me.
You are my rock and my protection.
For the good of your name, lead me and guide me.
Set me free from the trap they set for me.
You are my protection.
I give you my life.
Save me, Lord, God of truth.
    - Psalm 31:1-5

Heart to Heart Devotion

    This psalm is like so many of the other ones we have read in this book. It tells us that we can trust God because He saves us. He listens to us and He protects us. God loves you and does all these things because of He loves you. But He also does this, because God isn't able to not do these things to those who love Him. God leads those who love Him.

    This is the truth about God. God is truth, He is the God of truth. God leads you in His truth. You can trust your life with God forever.

     discipleshipstudio.com

Questions and Conversations

How is God, the God of truth?

How can you trust God with your life?

How do you think God leads and guides people?

Prayer Starters

God, You are ...

God, thank You ...

God, I pray ...

Creative Activity

Draw a picture of someone helping another person find their way in a forest.

Prayers Answered

Today's Date: ___________

God Forgives Me

Happy is the person
whose sins are forgiven,
whose wrongs are pardoned.
Happy is the person
whom the Lord does not consider guilty.
In that person there is nothing false.
     - Psalm 32:1-2

Heart to Heart Devotion

   Everyone sins. Sin is when we think or do something that God doesn't want us to think or do. God doesn't like sin at all. In fact, God hates sin. It's not a good to use such a strong word like hate when we think about other people, but it is a good word to describe how God feels about sin.

   God hates sin. He loves you. God rescues us from sin. He forgives us for the sin we think and do. We never want to make God unhappy because of our sin. Thanks to Jesus, we are forgiven from our sin. Jesus is the only one to live on earth and not sin. Jesus did this to make God happy. Since Jesus made God happy, God is happy to forgive us when we follow Jesus. When we are forgiven of the things we think or do that God doesn't want us to think or do, we are happy. Because of Jesus, God forgives you. Follow Jesus for your whole life.

          discipleshipstudio.com

Questions and Conversations

What is sin?

Why would someone who is forgiven from their sin be happy?

Prayer Starters

God, You are ...

God, thank You ...

God, I pray ...

Creative Activity

Draw a picture of someone happy because they have been forgiven from their sin.

Prayers Answered

My Big Prayers

Today's Date: _____________

God is Powerful

God's word is true.
Everything he does is right.
He loves what is right and fair.
The Lord's love fills the earth.
The sky was made at the Lord's command.
By the breath from his mouth, he made all the stars.
He gathered the water in the sea into a heap.
He made the great ocean stay in its place.
All the earth should worship the Lord.
The whole world should fear him.
He spoke, and it happened.
He commanded, and it appeared.
*   - Psalm 33:4-9*

Heart to Heart Devotion

When God created everything, He spoke it into existence. It's kind of like God saying, "cow" and then poof, a cow shows up. God didn't use anything to create. He didn't use clay or paint.

God made everything out of nothing. He spoke everything into existence. We can't say, "cow" and make a cow show up. God can. He can because He is powerful. He is wonderfully powerful. Because of that, we can praise God. You and I can praise the wonderfully powerful God who wonderfully created you and me.

     discipleshipstudio.com

Questions and Conversations

How did God make everything?

Can we make stars appear by using our voice?

How much more powerful is God than us?

Prayer Starters

God, You are ...

God, thank You ...

God, I pray ...

Creative Activity

Draw a picture of a mouth and then draw some stars around the mouth.

Prayers Answered

My Big Prayers

God Sees Everyone

Happy is the nation whose God is the Lord.
Happy are the people he chose for his very own.
The Lord looks down from heaven.
He sees every person.
From his throne he watches
everyone who lives on earth.
He made their hearts.
He understands everything they do.
Lord, show your love to us as we put our hope in
you.
    - Psalm 33:12-15, 22

Heart to Heart Devotion

    God can do things we cannot do. He can see everybody all the time. No one can hide from God. That's powerful. We don't know how He can do it; maybe it's like having a big screen television, where He watches us from, maybe it's all in His mind. Either way, God can see all of us all of the time.

    When He's watching us, He is caring for us. He is looking out for us. God is a good God who cares for those who love Him.

 discipleshipstudio.com

Questions and Conversations

Do you think it is good or bad that God can see every person?

How do you think God can see everything that a person does?

Prayer Starters

God, You are ...

God, thank You ...

God, I pray ...

Creative Activity

Draw a picture of people living on earth.

Prayers Answered

My Big Prayers

God is Great

I will praise the Lord at all times.
His praise is always on my lips.
My whole being praises the Lord.
The poor will hear and be glad.
Tell the greatness of the Lord with me.
Let us praise his name together.
I asked the Lord for help, and he answered me.
He saved me from all that I feared.
Those who go to him for help are happy.
They are never disgraced.
    - Psalm 34:1-5

Heart to Heart Devotion

    When we follow Jesus, we are to tell our friends, family, and everyone else about God. Some of the people we tell about God will need to hear about Him. When they hear about God, they will be happy, because they will find that God is what they have needed in their life.

    God will save some of the people you and I tell about Him. God is great. He is able to do great and mighty things. He does great things by using us. When we tell our friends, family, and others about God, we are able to praise God together with them. We are able to go tell others together about God. God is great and it is fun to tell others about the great things He does.

         discipleshipstudio.com

Questions and Conversations

How great is God? What are some great things He has done for us?

How can you praise God with your whole body?

Prayer Starters

God, You are ...

God, thank You ...

God, I pray ...

Creative Activity

Draw a picture of someone praising God with their body.

Prayers Answered

My Big Prayers

Today's Date: ___________

God Hears Me and Helps Me

This poor man called, and the Lord heard him.
The Lord saved him from all his troubles.
The Lord saves those who fear him.
His angel camps around them.
Examine and see how good the Lord is.
Happy is the person who trusts the Lord.
People who belong to the Lord, fear him!
Those who fear him will have everything they need.
Even lions may become weak and hungry.
But those people who go to the Lord for help will
have every good thing.
    - Psalms 34:6-10

Heart to Heart Devotion

   No matter how life is going, if it is good or if it is not good, God is good. God is with you. God hears you. He helps you when you need Him the most. He saves you from trouble and He protects you.

   When you need something, you can go to God and ask for His help. He will hear you if you are following Jesus. He will give you what is best for you. God is so good. It doesn't matter how strong you may be, God is stronger and can help you.

     discipleshipstudio.com

Questions and Conversations

Does God hear us when we pray?

How does God help people?

Prayer Starters

God, You are ...

God, thank You ...

God, I pray ...

Creative Activity

Draw a picture of a weak little lion and a strong big person.

Prayers Answered

My Big Prayers

God Saves Children

Children, come and listen to me.
I will teach you to worship the Lord.
You must do these things
to enjoy life and have many happy days.
You must not say evil things.
You must not tell lies.
Stop doing evil and do good.
Look for peace and work for it.
The Lord sees the good people.
He listens to their prayers.
    - Psalms 34:11-15

Heart to Heart Devotion

God loves kids like you. God loves you. He wants you to know Him and to follow Jesus. God promises to teach you things about Him. He wants the best for you and He knows the best for you is to follow Jesus.

God knows that kids make mistakes, they think and do things that God doesn't want them to do. Remember, this is called sin. God doesn't want you to sin, but He knows you will. Because God loves you, He will save you from your sin.

God saves you by sending Jesus. You are saved when you love and follow Jesus. Being saved by God is a great reason to worship God.

       discipleshipstudio.com

How can we learn to worship God?

Who does God save?

Prayer Starters

God, You are …

God, thank You …

God, I pray …

Creative Activity

Draw a picture of children worshipping God.

Prayers Answered

About Floyd Gary Pierce
Floyd Gary Pierce is the husband of Emily and the father of Lily and Ruby. He has spent over 20 years in church ministry, many of those years teaching teenagers and children. He holds a Master of Arts in Biblical and Theological Studies from Knox Theological Seminary and serves as the Senior Pastor of White Plains Baptist Church in Scottsville, Kentucky. Visit FloydGaryPierce.com for more.

About Discipleship Studio
Discipleship Studio provides Biblical resources for you to know and follow Jesus. Visit DiscipleshipStudio.com for more discipleship resources and to leave a review of this book.

About My Big Prayers
My Big Prayers are a series of devotional prayer journals to help parents and grandparents in family discipleship. This book is the first in the series with plans to release at least one new My Big Prayer Journal each year for the next several years. Visit DiscipleshipStudio.com for more.

Leave a Review
Please leave a review of this book at DiscipleshipStudio.com/review.

www.ingramcontent.com/pod-product-compliance
Lightning Source LLC
Chambersburg PA
CBHW011928050726

47591CB00009B/2387